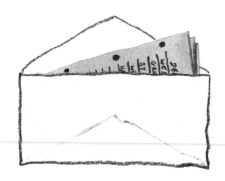

by Wallace J. Nichols & Wallace Grayce Nichols
illustrated by Drew Beckmeyer

cameron kids

Dear Wild Child,

We built your house
around you when you
were still growing inside
your mother, in the shade
of ancient redwood trees,
by a creek, not far from
the ocean.

We built your house stout and soulful to protect and raise you to be strong and healthy.

Hardwood and stone. Heavy truss and steel bolt. Knob and switch.

We never locked it. We didn't have to—
it never really belonged to us.

We filled it with books, guitars, a piano,
seashells, feathers, and animals.

And memories.

You learning to walk.
The wide, worn Douglas fir
floorboards holding you up.

Loving voices singing
sweet lullabies.

The wind singing through the canyon, the trees, and the chimney. The fireplace crackling and warming us as we slept.

Collecting eggs and cooking pancakes at dawn.

You growing taller and stronger like a little sapling.

In our canyon you discovered
salamanders, swimming holes,
fairy houses, buckets full of plums,
heart-shaped rocks, crawdads,
bright stars, and owl calls.

Your home grew brighter and wilder with people—great parties, friends' weddings, holiday gatherings, and sleepovers.

Hundreds of visitors, beautiful music, delicious dinners, and rich, deep conversations.

I had hoped this house would be yours someday.

Your home in the redwoods, by a creek,
not far from the ocean was as old as you were.

It stood strong through droughts, floods, and earthquakes.
You were there for it all.

Last night, the wildest, most beautiful
lightning storm I have ever seen blew
across the ocean and through our canyon.

The lightning ignited a wildfire. The
unstoppable flames roared over the ridges
and climbed the tall trees. The fire took
back your house.

I wish I could have protected it.
But I couldn't and I didn't.

All that remains standing is the ledgestone chimney
that still sings with the wind through the trees

Your house served its original purpose.
You are healthy and strong because of your home. It grew you.

You are made of hardwood and stone, bright stars, and the wind's song.
You are made of plums, Mill Creek water, and Pacific salmon.
You are made of sea salt, piano keys, and mountain lion screams.

Your house might be gone,
but you will carry your home
with you wherever you go.

You are my wild child.

# Love, Dad.

We built our home by hand twenty years ago, by a creek in the redwoods, in the wild region called the Slow Coast, north of Santa Cruz, California. We raised our two daughters here.

On the night of August 19, 2020, our house burned to the ground. A stunningly beautiful electrical storm, unlike anything we'd ever seen, had blown in from the Pacific Ocean. Eleven thousand bolts of lightning touched down across California, starting over six hundred wildfires, one of which became known as the CZU Lightning Complex fire. It burned across the ridges, through the oldest state park, home to five-hundred-year-old redwoods, and down the canyons of the Santa Cruz Mountains where we lived.

There was only enough time to throw a few things into a duffel bag, grab our dog, George, jump into the Jeep, and head south. Just the day before, our oldest daughter, Wallace Grayce, had left home for her first year of college on the East Coast. I called her the next morning to tell her that the only home she'd ever known had burned to the ground. She began to cry, and I wrote her a letter.

The climate is changing. Weather is becoming less predictable and more extreme. We will lose what we love. And to fix what's broken, we will all need to become resilient and more empathetic, collaborative, and creative. The redwood forests may be our best teacher.

Our desconstructed Slow Coast home in the redwoods, by a creek, not far from the ocean now consists of six low-impact solar-powered platform tents called Jupes, a mobile sauna trailer, and outdoor shower. We look forward to inviting friends and family to visit again and stay awhile.

To Ben and Jan Wilson — W.J.N. & W.G.N.

For Pegleg — D.B.

## WANT TO HELP?

The organization *After the Fire* advocates
for communities impacted by megafires and
better forest management.
For more information, see www.afterthefireusa.org.

Text © 2022 Wallace J. Nichols and Wallace Grayce Nichols
Illustrations © 2022 Drew Beckmeyer

Book design by Melissa Nelson Greenberg

Library of Congress Cataloging-in-Publication Data available.
ISBN: 978-1-951836-46-7

Printed in China

10 9 8 7 6 5 4 3 2 1

CAMERON KIDS is an imprint of CAMERON + COMPANY

**CAMERON + COMPANY**
Petaluma, California
www.cameronbooks.com

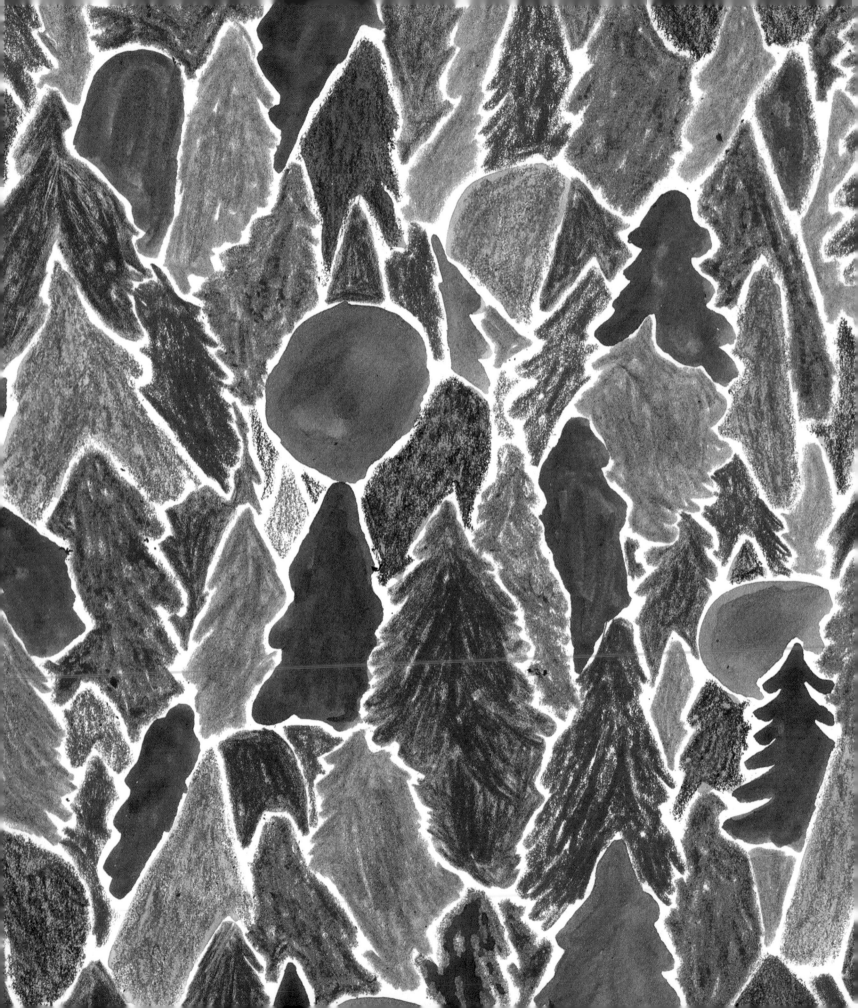